# Praise for UPROOTED

"Ruth Chan tells her story of international upheaval with charming cartooning, pitch-perfect humor, and tons of heart. I loved every salty-sweet moment."

—VERA BROSGOL, creator of *Be Prepared* and the *New York Times* bestseller *Anya's Ghost*

"When the world around you feels out of your control, this book is a grounding force. Ruth's tender, profoundly funny, and well-earned insights will give readers the courage to approach the uncertainties of life with excitement. I loved every moment."

—CHANEL MILLER, *New York Times*–bestselling author of *Know My Name*

"UPROOTED is more than just a coming-of-age story. The beauty of Ruth Chan's memoir comes from her finding truth in the quietest of moments and strength in the toughest times."

—LEUYEN PHAM, *New York Times*–bestselling co-creator of the Friends graphic novel series

"Kids and adults will both adore and relate to this wonderful memoir about Ruth's real-life struggle to adapt and fit into a new home."

—DAN SANTAT, Caldecott Medalist and creator of the National Book Award winner *A First Time for Everything*

"Through vivid detail and earnest recollection, readers young and old will be transported into Ruth Chan's world. A sweet and honest love letter to a family and the city of Hong Kong."

—JEN WANG, author of *Stargazing* and *The Prince and the Dressmaker*

To
Hong Kong,
and to all
my friends
and family
there.

Published by Roaring Brook Press • Roaring Brook Press is a division of Holtzbrinck Publishing Holdings Limited Partnership • 120 Broadway, New York, NY 10271 • mackids.com



Our books may be purchased in bulk for promotional, educational, or business use. Please contact your local bookseller or the Macmillan Corporate and Premium Sales Department at (800) 221-7945 ext. 5442 or by email at MacmillanSpecialMarkets@macmillan.com.

Library of Congress Control Number: 2023948830

First edition, 2024
Color by Niccolo Pizarro

Printed in Malaysia by RR Donnelley Asia Printing Solutions Ltd., Seberang Perai, Penang

ISBN 978-1-250-85533-6 (hardcover)
1 3 5 7 9 10 8 6 4 2

ISBN 978-1-250-85534-3 (paperback)
1 3 5 7 9 10 8 6 4 2

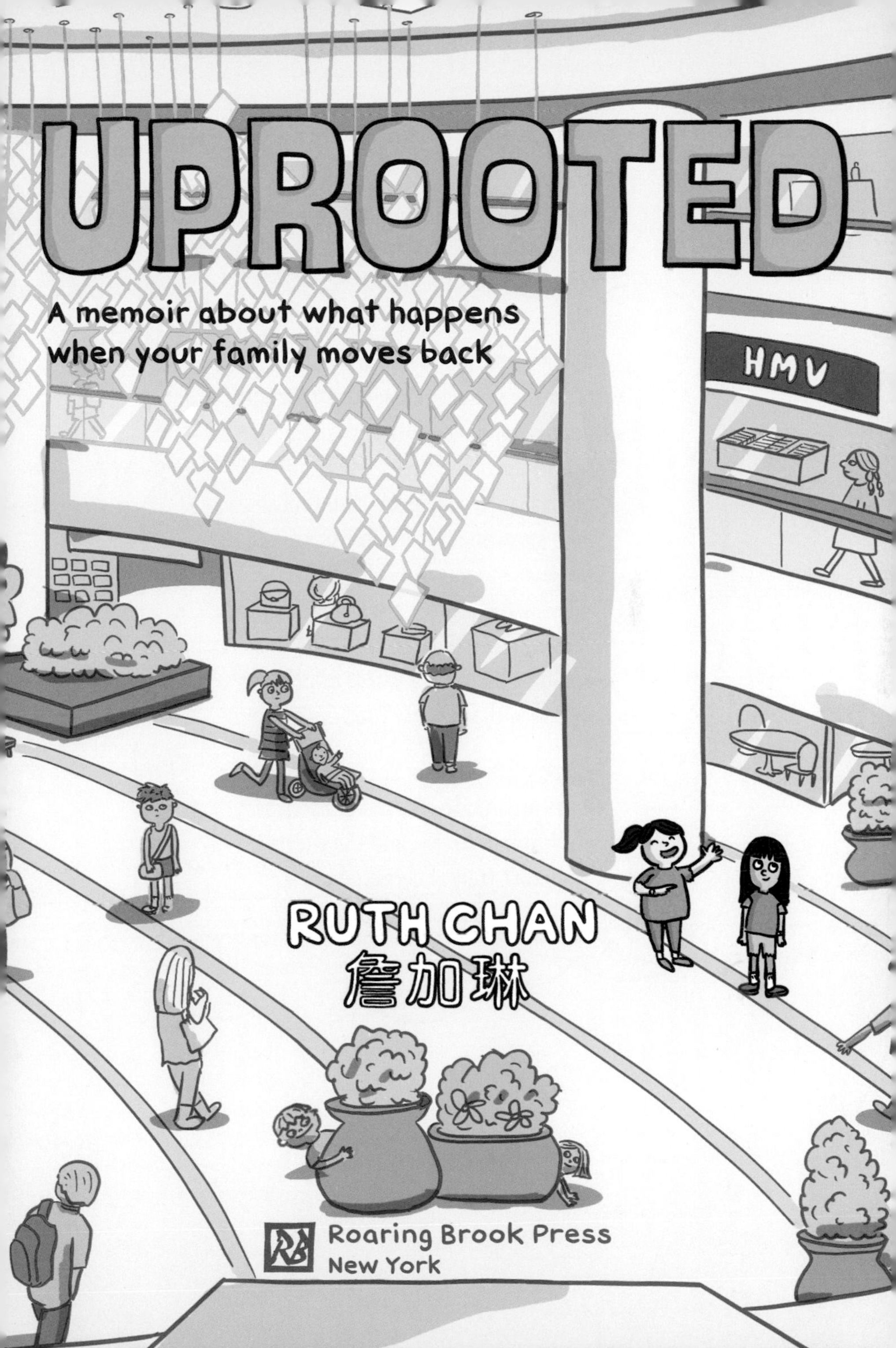


# UPROOTED

A memoir about what happens when your family moves back

RUTH CHAN

詹加琳

Roaring Brook Press
New York

Like a lot of kids who grew up in English-speaking countries with parents who spoke languages other than English, I grew up speaking both English and my parents' native language, Cantonese. More specifically, my parents spoke Cantonese to me, and I spoke English to them. Sometimes they would mix Cantonese and English together, and sometimes there were words or phrases in Cantonese that I didn't fully understand.

To make this clear for you, the English words are in **black,** the Cantonese words are in gray, and the words I couldn't fully understand are in Chinese characters.

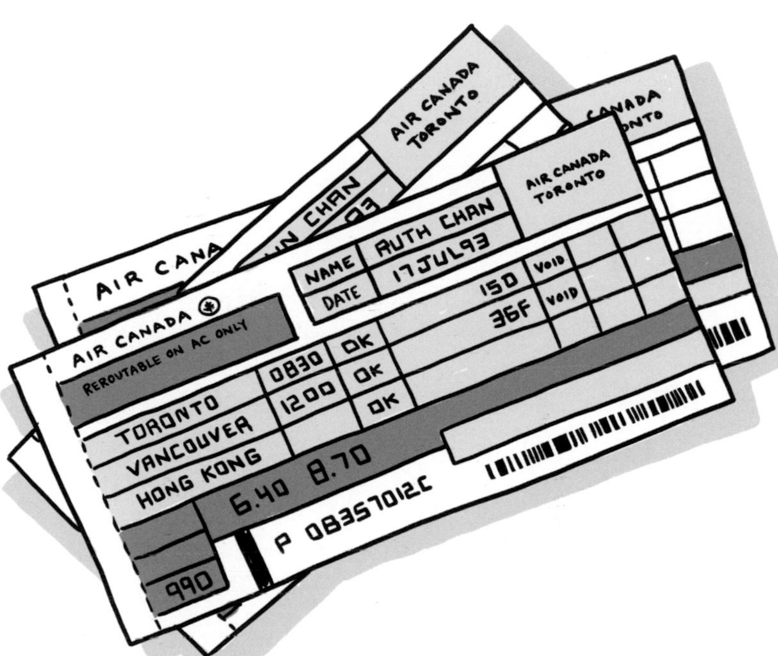
AIR CANADA
TORONTO
AIR CANADA
TORONTO
AIR CANADA
TORONTO
NAME
RUTH CHAN
DATE
17JUL93
15D
VOID
36F
VOID
AIR CANADA
REROUTABLE ON AC ONLY
0830
OK
1200
OK
OK
TORONTO
VANCOUVER
HONG KONG
6.40
8.70
990
P 08357012C

CHAPTER 1

TORONTO 1993

I wish this day would never end.
The MIGHTY CANADIAN
MINEBUSTER

I'm at my favorite place in the world...
Ruth!

...with my favorite people...
Earth to Ruth!

Huh?

We're almost there!

...doing one of my favorite things.

Wow, you can see all of Toronto from up here.
The tiny airport on that empty field with the cute name. Buttonham? Buttonville?
And there's the mall Mom and I hang out at while waiting for my brother to finish his cello lessons.
And there's our school where, most importantly, I had my first kiss behind the playground.

Ugh. And
in two days, I'll be
leaving it all.

For a whole
new country.

That was crazy! I almost peed myself!
Let's go again!
Let's go on The Bat instead! It goes backward!

Ruth, what do you want to do?

Let's get ice cream first!
YES!

OK, a little rewind. The first thing you should know about me is that I LOVE ice cream.
I could eat it for breakfast, lunch, and dinner.

The second thing you should know about me is that I have the best friends in the world.

Yum!

OMG, you need a napkin!

Now we'll stay friends FOREVER!

AHHHHH

There they are!

In the still of the night...

Ugh, Ruth! I'm going to miss you SO much!
Me too. I can't believe you're moving all the way to Hong Kong.
I know! I can't even imagine life without you guys!

I know them so well.
...And who's going to tell me to talk to boys even when I'm nervous?
And, like, who's going to watch *Jurassic Park* with me?!
EXIT

You can write us letters about Hong Kong, and we'll write you about everything going on here.
We'll still be "us," don't worry!

There's your mom.
And your dad.
CANADA'S
WONDERLA

This is really it...

PICK
UP

We'll see you before you know it!

I'll write every day!

Wahhhh!

Bye, Ruth!

BYE!

Love you!

I'm going to miss them.
And this.
Church (mostly my friends)
And this.
SAM SAM
SAM THE RECORD MAN
Shopping Yonge Street
Definitely this.
COUNTRY STYLE DONUTS
Favorite snack spot
Piano teacher's house
Okay, maybe not that.

How was your day, Mui*?
*Mui = "little sister" in Cantonese, aka my nickname
It was fun.

Good. Because you have a lot of packing to do when we get home.
And you should speak in Cantonese to practice.

It seems like the only thing we talk about these days is The Move.

And don't forget tomorrow. You have to...

And then we have to take your brother...

I've only been to Hong Kong once, when I was five, and all I remember is...

Almost all of my mom's family is in Hong Kong, but all I know about them is that they talk REALLY LOUD.

In Cantonese.

Which I understand but can barely speak.

So, yeah. Big change.

It's hard to imagine what life will be like.

Will it look the same?

Will it feel the same?
55

Okay, so go change, then pack your room, and then help pack the kitchen.

We're HOME!

Ah, home! Where everyone and everything belongs.
Where my shoes belong.

Where I belong.

Where TV makes sense.

Where Goh* can be found in front of the TV. All. The. Time.
I can smell you from here.
*Goh = "big brother" in Cantonese

You mean like fun and laughter and joy?
Okay, enough. You both have packing to do.

It pains me to pack up my room—it's so GLORIOUS!
Aladdin
ALOMAR
NEW KIDS ON THE BLOCK
HUGE windows!
Posters I have painstakingly arranged over and over.
Ruth
Radio and tape deck to record songs for my friends.
My own bathroom! I know! It's like I'm living the life of a movie star.
Hannibal!
Pot of Gold
Desk where I journal/daydream.
My weirdo cat, Kitty. (I named him when I was a little kid.)
Farewell present from my best friends.
Ru!

Where to start? How do you just pack up your LIFE?

Will I even need sweaters there?

Can't forget this.
ADA'S WONDER

Or my rock collection.

Or my eraser collection.

Or my keychain collection.
KEYCHA

Need my baseball card collection.

Can't live without my pig collection.

I wish she didn't have to move.
She won't have any friends.
She barely even speaks Cantonese!
And her brother won't even be there, and her dad will be gone a LOT.

Dad!
Hi!

I like this kind of enthusiastic welcome!

Looks like you had some fun in the sun!
I did!

Okay, you two. Go wash your hands.

And your dad needs to change.

Yum, my favorite! Steamed fish!
Okay, Goh, you pray.
Ugh, fine.

Dear God, thank you for the food and let's eat. Amen.
And for this time we have together as a family. Amen.

Shall we go over the Pros and Cons list?

Dad loves lists. He's organized like that.
Maybe it'll change their minds about going.
Isn't it too late?

I feel like my contribution to the Con side is pretty important. Just sayin'.

I REALLY think it's too late, guys.

PROS AND CONS OF MOVING TO HONG KONG (except Wes)

| PROS | CONS |
| --- | --- |
| 1. Good job for dad | 1. Leaving Goh (in boarding school) |
| 2. Good school for me (Mui) | 2. Leaving EVERYTHING! |
| 3. Mom close to family | |

It's still helpful. So we feel good about our decision.

Yes! I feel good about it.

The next day, we drop Goh off at his boarding school.
Got enough stuff, Goh?
Just my entire LIFE.

He's not coming to Hong Kong since he only has one year of school left.
So, when will we see you next?
Christmas. I think I'm coming to Hong Kong.
Yes, you are coming for Christmas.

Plus, he loves his school, and all his friends are here.
Do you have everything?
Well... Um...
Yeah, I think so.
UCC

Mom is so sad, and Goh pretends like he doesn't care.
Make sure you eat enough.
Yeah, okay. I'll see you soon.

And I suddenly realize, whoa, I kind of care.
UCC
See you at Christmas...

I'm going to go finish packing.
Good.

I think Goh will miss us.

And yep. I weirdly kind of miss him already.

My favorite Blue Jays player!

RING! RING!
I'll get it!

Phone! I'll get it!
RING!

Probably for me anyway!

Hello! Chan family residence this is Ruth speaking and to whom am I speaking?

Oh, hey, Grace! I knoooow. I already miss you too.

It's going to be weird not talking on the phone. Stupid long-distance costs.

Okay, I should go too...
Bye.

I'll admit, as much as I don't want to leave, I'm glad I'm going with Mom and Dad. I'd be freaking out if they left me here in some school by myself.
STUFFED ANIMALS

I wonder if I'll feel like an only child. I'll get all the attention! All the things!
Wait.
All the nagging too.
STUFFED ANIMALS

Mui, are you all done? You should go to bed. The movers are coming early.

Speaking of nagging...
Yes, I'm done. But Dad and I are going to have a Talk-to-Talk tonight.
Okay, but you guys don't keep it going too late.

KETS
CLOTHES
STUFFED ANIMALS
DIARIES + BOOKS
DESK STUFF
MORE PIGS
PIGGIES

Whoa.

It's really happening.

What is Talk-to-Talk?
Let me explain!
THE HISTORY OF TALK-TO-TALK

It all started when Dad got tired of reading stories.
Toilet. Toothbrush. Bathtub.
Pin-cushion. Ruler. Iron.

Okay, it's very hard to read a Richard Scarry book out loud.
Richard Scarry's BEST

How about we talk about how our days were?

Okay!
Let's call it... Talk-to-Talk.

Yeah! And we'll just talk and stuff!

My dad's always been pretty quiet, so it was basically ME talking 90% of the time for years and years.
Daddy! Jordan hit his head on the table and he laughed and then he turned around and there was blood EVERYWHERE and it was so cool!
I can barely feel it.
That's a LOT of blood!
Oh. Wow. Okay.

Even when we talked about nonsense...
Dad, how are ice skates made?
Well...there's an alligator wearing oven mitts who glues the blade onto the shoe...
Are you sure?

...or stuff he wouldn't want to hear.
So we made taffy in French class and I ate it all but then I threw up!
Tirer
Not my finest moment, but it was just too good to stop!

Sometimes we didn't talk at all.
Talk-to-Talk has always been kind of OUR thing.

Maybe it's our thing because Dad always falls asleep...
Psst. Daddy?
snore
...and never makes it to Goh's room.

Now? It'll be our last Talk-to-Talk here.

And the last night I'm brushing my teeth in this bathroom.

And turning off this light switch.
Wow. Never thought I'd be sad over a light switch.

This is the last time I'm getting into this bed too.

Sometimes it feels a little silly to still do Talk-to-Talks.
Dad?

I wonder if they'll change with Dad being in China most of the time.
Are you coming?

Have you ever thought that maybe I'm too old for this? Or your back is too old for it?

Nonsense! Talk-to-Talk has no age limit!

CRACK!

CRIK

There's a lot going on this week, eh?

Oh, like that tiny thing called MOVING ACROSS THE WORLD?

I like to think of it as starting a new family adventure!

A family adventure minus Goh!

Well, he's going to be having his own adventure.

So...I have something I want to talk to you about.

Uh-oh...

Dad initiating talking? In English?

This isn't going to be fun, is it...

What about?

Well, I'm going to tell it again. Ahem.

In 1944, before I was born, China was in the midst of the Sino-Japanese War. Your grandfather was a customs officer, and our family lived in a customs compound in Southern China, in a town called Wuzhou.

Your grandmother was six months pregnant with me...

...when your uncle, who was two years old, made a prophecy.

The Japanese are coming.

We need to leave tomorrow.

There were rumors the Japanese soldiers were invading nearby.

After your uncle prophesied, they turned on the radio.

He was right.

So they did.

They packed two blankets, two sets of clothes, and two flashlights.
Keep these safe. They are your responsibility. Can I count on you?
Yes.

Your grandmother was put on a sedan chair.

The whole complex gathered in the courtyard.
Everyone ready? Let's go.

They left in the darkness of night.
Where are we going?
I don't know yet, but we'll start by heading up into those mountains.

They climbed and climbed.
I...can't... walk anymore.

HUFF PUFF

They said goodbye to their home...
...and set off into the unknown.

And then?

Eh?

Where did they end up going?

You already know the story!

Sure, but you can't just stop the story at the suspenseful part!

But I can. I'm your father.

In all seriousness, there's a reason why the story of how I was born keeps getting told and passed on in our family.

I know the story, but it feels different when you're telling it this time. Like it's more real or something.
I know this move is becoming more real too. By our next Talk-to-Talk, we'll have said goodbye to our home here and hello to our new one.

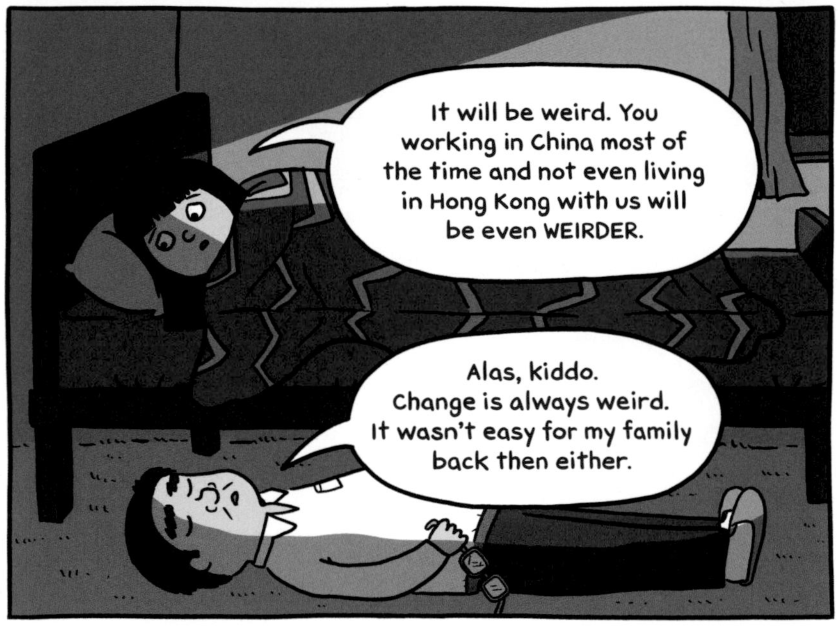
It will be weird. You working in China most of the time and not even living in Hong Kong with us will be even WEIRDER.
Alas, kiddo. Change is always weird. It wasn't easy for my family back then either.

It's okay to be nervous about change and the unknown. Just remember that you'll be okay. The unknown is simply a part of life.

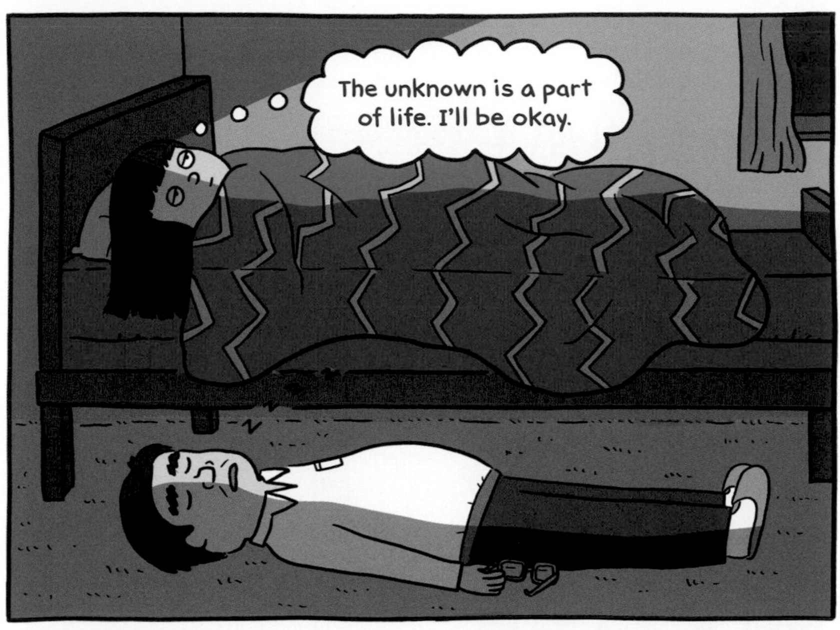
The unknown is a part
of life. I'll be okay.

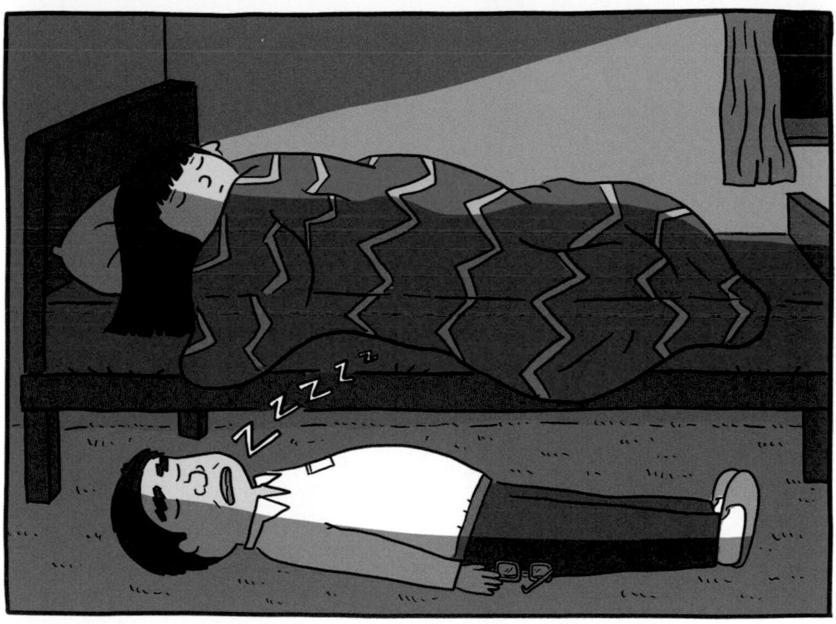
Z Z Z Z Z z

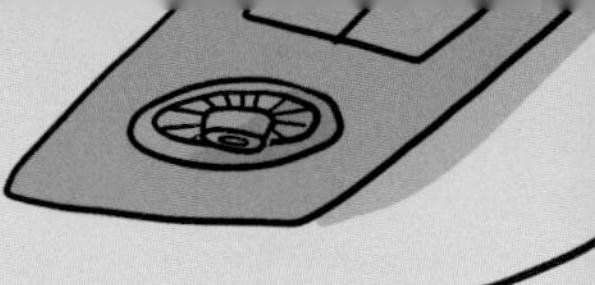

# CHAPTER 2

Usually, I like plane rides.
Ruth

Because they give you an excuse to do nothing.

But this one is SO long.
...flying time is 15 hours, so sit back and relax...

2 hours in
747

4 hours in

? hours in?!

You will always be our Babe Ruth. Nothing can change that. We miss you and love you! ♥

BIENVENUE
BEAVERTAILS
CINNAMON SUGAR
CINNAMON SUGAR + LEMON
CRACK!

Byeee!

POP!
Mui! Wake up. We're here!

WHOA.

There's so much of... everything!

OMG. We're gonna hit a building!

SCREECH

Welcome to Hong Kong, Ruth. Your new home.

Where people are everywhere.
WELCOME TO HONG KONG
歡迎蒞臨香港

And all look like...me?
入境檢查 A
IMMIGRATION B
入境檢查 C
IMMIGRATION D

CUSTOMS
Quick! Grab the black one!
Which black one?

And are all yelling in Cantonese.
Yes!
Hey!
我喺呢度!
Hi!
快啲啦!
Coming!
OK!

Kitty!
Hannibal!
You guys
made it!

There are lines for everything.
HONG KONG
EXIT 出口
There's a line
to exit?!

TAXI
It's so
HOT here!
Hopefully
the taxi line
will move
quickly.
It's called a
"queue" here.
TAXI

TAXI
TAXI
Why's the
driver on
that side?

出口
EXIT
的士
TAXI

People are driving on the wrong side of the road!

TAXI
KODAK
DB 7148

OK, I do NOT remember Hong Kong being THIS chaotic.
My sisters and I used to go shopping here all the time!
It's so... LOUD.

My favorite congee place was near here. I wonder if it's still around!
TRAM

So many mountains.
Wow! Lots of new buildings have gone up!
的士

And there are more buildings IN the mountains?!

TOWER 7
This is us!

TOWER 7
Welcome home!
We're on the 15th floor. Let's go up!
I'm still dizzy from driving on the wrong side of the road.

APT 1547

My new home. Wow. Does NOT feel real.
Who does all this furniture belong to?
It's ours! Dad's company is lending it to us.

This must be my new room.

Whoa. You can see everything from up here.

And now to make this room MY room.
PIGS

OK, new life, meet my old life.

It's funny how all these familiar things are now part of my OLD life.

They look kind of weird in this new place. Like they don't belong here or something.

At least you guys are still the same.

DAY 1
OK, wow. Maybe I COULD get used to this?

DAY 2
You still have so much to unpack!
Jet...lag... so...tired.

DAY 3
Did you look at your school materials list yet?
But you just said I need to unpack!

DAY 4
What happened to just normal chips?
No junk food. Let's go.

DAY 5
Be careful with those plates.

DAY 6
Finally, a break!

DAY 7
Let's go! Poh Poh* and Gong Gong* are waiting.
*Poh Poh = Grandma on my mom's side
*Gong Gong = Grandpa on my mom's side

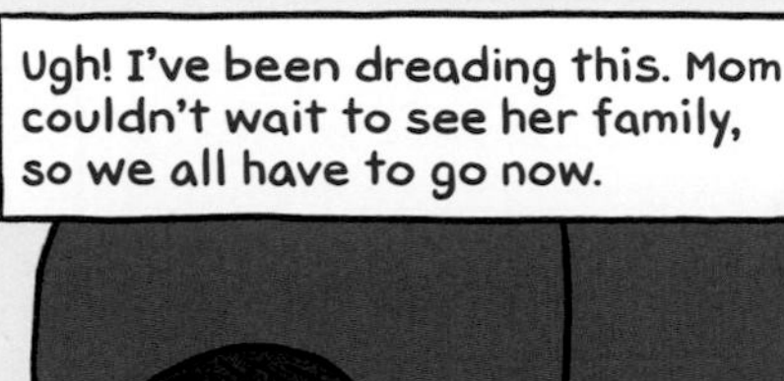
Ugh! I've been dreading this. Mom couldn't wait to see her family, so we all have to go now.

Everyone's going to be there, and I don't even remember who's who.
I don't feel well, so, um...maybe I should stay home.
Excuses! Let's go!

Everyone ready? My family is waiting for us to start eating!
I think she's pretty excited.
Hurry up!
You think?!

After you...
Thanks.

Don't forget the gift!

Of course not.

出口 EXIT
OK. I've never doubted Mom's driving in Canada, but all of a sudden, this is super freaky.
Don't forget to greet everyone by their names in order of seniority.
If we even make it. Hee hee.
Heh!
Why are you laughing at me with your daughter?!

I very vaguely remember Poh Poh and Gong Gong's building.
輝永大廈 FAIR WIND MANOR

Good afternoon!
Good afternoon!

SCHOOM

2

3
PING
We're here!

3
SWOOSH

筷子喺邊度?
We're out of toilet paper!
HA HA HA HA HA

Oh. My. Crap.
Welcome to Hong Kong! And to Poh Poh and Gong Gong's!
Um... H-h-hello, everyone...
Ah Mui! You are growing into a beautiful woman!
好耐冇見你啦!
你同你老竇一樣樣!

How's your Chinese?

A Chinese girl should speak Chinese.

I can understand... But speaking not...um... so good.

HA HA HA HA HA HA HA HA
好可愛啊
HA HA

I swear, I try to make her speak Cantonese at home, but she REFUSES!
OMG.

Hi, Ruth! How do you like Hong Kong so far?
Um... It's OK... I guess.

And...?
Um...

Please, ground, just swallow me up.

I can't get anyone straight either.
THE Li Family Tree
Poh Poh
Gong Gong
Mom
Yeema*
Another yeema
And another yeema?
An uncle (kau fu?)
Another uncle
Lost track
No idea
I feel crazy
Angie
Me
Goh
NOT EVEN GONNA TRY
* Yeema = any older sister of Mom's
TIME TO FEAST!

Beef Chow Fun
WIDE RICE NOODLE
GREEN ONION + ONION
BEEF
SOY SAUCE
BEAN SPROUTS
Tea
Singapore Fried Noodle
RICE VERMICELLI
BBQ PORK
BEAN SPROUTS
SCRAMBLED EGG
GREEN ONION
SHRIMP
CURRY POWDER
Watermelon
Hainanese Chicken
Steamed Pork Buns
JUICY PIECES OF BBQ PORK
FLUFFY BUN
SWEET SAVORY SAUCE
Yeung Chow Fried Rice
RICE
PORK
SHRIMP
PEAS
SCRAMBLED EGG

Finally! Something I understand!
YUM YUM YUM
YUM YUM YUM
YUM YUM YUM

Psst. We need to invite the elders to eat before anyone starts.

Elders, please eat!

冇問題。佢唔知道係冇禮貌.
Could this day possibly get any worse?

你哋仔囡
in the West
長大就會噉樣.
They forget respect. And Chinese values.
There are many new things she has to learn.

It's like I'm not even here.

Like I'm some stranger to them.

No one is going to even notice if I just sneak away.

If I don't even fit in with my family, how am I supposed to fit in anywhere?!

RD ROCK
AFE

HA HA HA HA HA HA HA HA HA
HA HA HA

HA HA HA

SCRATCH
SCRITCH
SCRATCHY
SCRITCH

Hey there, little guy.

MEW

Didn't want to join the party?

Kind of stuck here, eh?

MEOW

HA HA
HA HA

A few nights later...
Heading to bed?

Yeah. First day of school tomorrow.
9:00pm is a little early, no?

I have to get up at 5:30!
I think there's time for a little Talk-to-Talk tonight though.

The first one in a new place. Got to have some consistency, eh?
The ONE consistent thing...

Don't forget, I'm going to China for work tomorrow.
Oh yeah.

I wish you didn't have to go...

It was so embarrassing at Poh Poh's.

Like no one wanted to be with me because I wasn't Chinese enough or something.

How am I going to fit into a new school—a GERMAN one—when I can't even fit in with family?!

I know that was tough, but you'll be fine.
It always takes time to feel comfortable in any new situation, even at the best school In Hong Kong.

Our family climbed through the mountains for weeks along with the rest of the compound.

We don't know how close the Japanese are.

We just have to keep going...

They rested as little as possible to avoid being captured...
Just a little farther till we can stop.
...and ate what they could find...
Eat these leaves, they'll give you energy.
But there are bugs on them.
...until they finally came upon a village.

Look! Let's go down.
What if it is already invaded?

Looks like it's OK, or it would have been plundered.

So they descended into the valley...

...until they arrived at the village of Pang Fa.

My father was so relieved, he had to sit in the paddy fields outside the village to weep.

When he recovered, the family followed the others into the village.

And tried to find...

...a place to stay.

But no matter where they went...
Any space would do.

...they were rejected.
SLAM

When they asked why, villagers said...
Your wife will give birth soon, and blood is unlucky. We cannot afford to risk having bad fortune put on us, especially during a war.

So they kept asking and looking until they had gone through the whole village.

Unwilling to give up, my mother suggested they look on the outskirts of the village.

But they finally ran into some good fortune.

It was a kind doctor.

You can't be running around in your condition.

Nor your children.

She wanted to help this tired and starving family.

And she led them to the one place she could think of.

You can stay here as long as you need.

It's not much, but it's a roof over your heads.
Yes, thank you so much.

This is our new home for now, kids!

I know it's not ideal.

But be patient, and it will become more comfortable.

And soon, we'll find where we belong.

The fact that they had to live in a BARN always blows my mind.
Yep. With a full pigsty.

But it's amazing how quickly you can get used to something that was once uncomfortable.
I found rice!
The pigs are snorting. So cute!

Pigs are cute. I could be patient with a pig.

YAWN

SWEEP

6:30 is way too early to be waiting at a bus stop. I can't remember the last time I woke up so early...if ever?
How are they so... awake?

Ugh, I should have eaten more breakfast.

First day of school. Breathe, Ruth.
DEUTSCH-SCHWEIZERISCHE INTERNATIONALE SCHULE
GERMAN SWISS INTERNATIONAL SCHOOL
德瑞國際學校
GSIS

Here goes nothing...

Hallo!
Einfach Klasse!
I missed you!

KLASSENZIMMER
101-112
3-120

KLASSENZIMMER
101-112

KLASSENZIMMER
101 - 112
113-

KLASSENZIMMER
BADEZIMMER
101
102
103B
TURNHALLE
104
105
106
107
108
?!

New here, are we?

Um... Yeah...

OK, so you're going to take the stairs here down two floors, and then you can wait down there.

OK.
Be cool.

BE COOL.

BE! COOL!

Er, excuse me, coming through.
Sure thing!

Hands in pockets. So cool.

Who walks down stairs like this?!

CATCH
TRIP
SILENT SCREAM
Whoa. Careful.
Are you OK?

Just...sit... down, Ruth.

Okayyyyy, soooo... Do I introduce myself to people?
Or do I just smoothly insert myself into a group?

I wonder what my friends in Toronto are doing...

Back to looking cool...
Looking like I just don't care.
Yup. So cool.

Sigh.

This school is so big!

Yeah. It is.

I'm Bonnie!

I'm Ruth!

Are you
new here?

Yup.
Are you?

Yeah!
Me too.

Do you want to be best friends?
Um... OK!
Cool!

I lived in Hong Kong until three years ago when we moved to Australia. Now I'm back. You?
I'm from Canada and have never lived anywhere else.

I've got a
FIFI.
Cute! I have a
HANNIBAL.

Cool! We have so much in common!

Wow. I made...a friend? Already? That was easy.

Totally.

I hate math. Hope it's not boring.
I don't mind it. I'm pretty good at it.

I've kind of been looking forward to math class.
Should we go in?
I guess so?

Ugh. First row seats. The new kids spot.
Welcome to maths.
Maths? Does he mean "math"?

Let's dive right into trigonometry.
Trigo-what?!

So sinØ= Opposite/ Hypotenuse.

Roof? Answer?
Er, it's Ruth.
Yes, Roof. Can you give us the answer?

Stay calm. If sinØ is... WHAT THE HECK IS sinØ?!
OK. Just focus.

Um.

I...

...don't...

...know.

And after maths is chemistry (which I've never had before).

And now the aluminium will act.

Does she mean aluminum?

And now GERMAN?!

Deutsch 1

Ich

Du

Guten Tag. Ich heisse Frau Yeoman und Ich habe einen Hund. Und dir?

W. H. A. T. ?!

I USED to like PE...

Grab your badminton rackets!

Why is the racket so small?

What a crazy first day! At least Crime Story comes out tomorrow!
Crime what?

Are you talking about the new Jackie Chan movie?
Yeah!
I THINK I know who that is.

I heard it's more serious than the first.
Based on a true story!
It's going to be SO good!
Sounds cool.

I prefer his funny stuff.
And his signature moves.
And his "ouch" face!
OK. No idea what's going on.

It's only 12pm, and I am wiped!
He's the best!
Totally.
Why do I feel like I was born yesterday?

CHAPTER 3
RING!
RING!

It's been two weeks, and I still feel like I'm just figuring things out.

Can you get that? It might be your father.

Why does it buzz twice?!

RING RING

But my Chinese sucks!
RIN

Like I said, it's probably your father. Just ANSWER IT!

UGH.

RING!
RING!

H-h-hello?

你好，詹先生
喺唔喺屋企？

MOM!

Literally my greatest nightmare.
It's for Dad, but the man's talking in Chinese. Can you take it... PLEASE?!

I'm busy. Tell him he's out of town.

Hello...

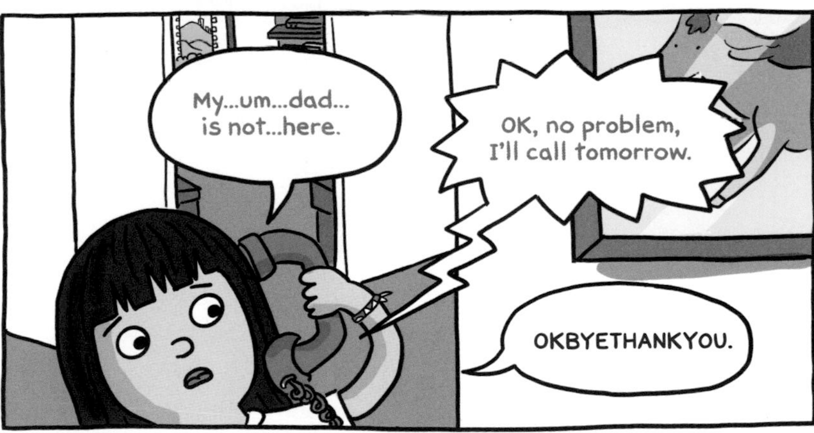
My...um...dad... is not...here.
OK, no problem, I'll call tomorrow.
OKBYETHANKYOU.

Who was it?
I dunno. Not Dad.

You need to get more comfortable with your Cantonese.
What's for dinner? Looks great. Let's eat.

I knew Dad being gone a lot would be weird, but, MAN, I wish he was here, even just to get a break from the nagging!

How are you going to get comfortable here if you are always scared to speak Cantonese?

And why are you being so SHY?

This is not like you at all.

I always said we should have made you speak Cantonese back to us.
Ugh. As if I don't already feel bad enough.

It's not like I WANT to be bad at Cantonese...

It all just feels really hard, and I'm not quite...
Oh! Did I tell you your yeema is going to take me to the market tomorrow? I can get you some new pants!
WHICH yeema? Like it matters.
What's wrong with my pants...?

I'm going to go do my homework.

One week of school, and there's already so much of it. SIGH.
8.6. STRUCTURES OF

So you're saying the rest of our things won't be here for another FOUR weeks?

SIGH.

RING
RING

Hello?

Oh, hi, sis! Yes, 10 o'clock works tomorrow! Can't wait.
And afternoon tea after shopping? Sure!
I'm trying to do work here...

YAWN
I wonder if that place in 中環 still has those egg tarts we used to love. They do? Great!

Yes!
Let's do that.

And then we can go see
that place with the...

SLAM!

I have a friend! (But no one compares to you guys.)

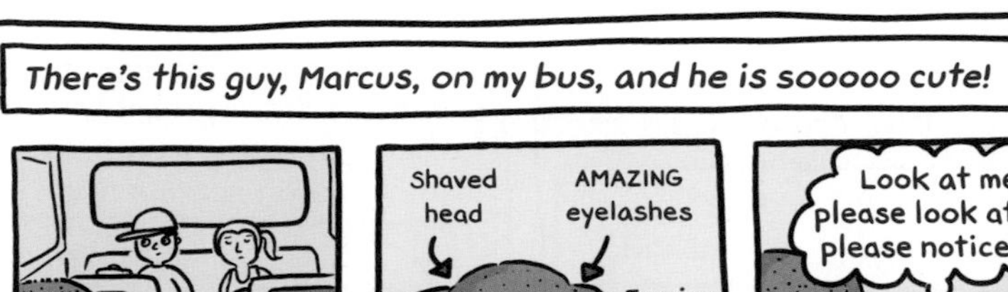
There's this guy, Marcus, on my bus, and he is sooooo cute!

Shaved head
AMAZING eyelashes
Earring (so cool!)

Look at me, please look at me, please notice me!

No one here plays baseball, so when we did for PE, I made this killer catch, and everyone was SO impressed, and I was kind of like a hero.
(Basically like this.)

I think I might be making friends with this other girl, Claudia, who is super sweet.
Do you want to be lab partners?
Yes!

Also, there's this OTHER really cute guy, Nick, and Bonnie and I are totally obsessed with him.
Cute spiky hair
Stüssy shirt
Skateboard
TEE HEE HEE

HERE ARE THINGS I DON'T LIKE:
Chemistry (like, the subject). I don't get any of it at all!
Also German class. Everyone seems to be better at it than I am.

To top it off, my mom is already nagging me about doing well in school.
Blah blah nag nag.

We have coed swimming for PE. It's SO. AWKWARD.
POOL SAFETY
CENSORED
CENSORED

My dad is always out of town, and my mom is busy loving her life here. Makes me miss my BROTHER of all people.

out of
my BROTHER of
I miss you guys the
I feel so far away
I am!) Write
♥
RUTH

I hope that's enough stamps.

One more list to finish...

RUTH'S GOALS!

Get Marcus (or Nick) (or both!) to notice me.

Learn all the names of my relatives so I can greet them the next time I see them so they don't hate me or think I'm a fool.

Find (and keep) some really good friends here.

It's finally the weekend, and Bonnie and I are finally hanging out.

I can't believe Mom let me come by myself.
I was worried about getting lost, so I left extra early.

Is there another McDonald's I'm supposed to be at?

RUTH!

Hi, Bonnie!

Sorry I'm late, I hope you weren't waiting long.
Nope, not at all!

Welcome to Pacific Place! Where all our teenage dreams come true!
LOFT
88

There's a movie theater
with cheap tickets
on Tuesdays!
There's Benetton,
Bossini, U2, Esprit, and
Hang Ten. Basically all
your fashion needs!
Jumbo B Grade for
cute erasers and
pens galore!

There's The Body Shop for lotions and perfumes, and a bookstore with MORE stationery!
HMV
Ooh, and Hong Kong Records and HMV for all the music!
And the FOOD COURT! There's food from all over the world, and it has anything you're craving.
Ooh! Let's go there!

Pizza Hut
大家樂
Curry-in-a-Hurry
FOOD COURT
Holy moly. You weren't kidding.
Right?!

美心
What're you in the mood for?
Hmm. I'm kind of thirsty...

大家樂
CAFÉ DE CORAL
They have the best milk tea.
Ooh, I love milk tea.

茶餐
Hello! What would you like?
$25
$28

I'd like a 鴛鴦 please.
BOSS

迷你飯茶飯
Great! And you?
$28

Ummmm...

Do you want
紅荳冰,
凍好立克,
定係凍檸茶?

One cup...of...
um...iced milk...
**uh, tea.**

Sure thing!
No problem!

Wow! I ordered in Cantonese! That wasn't so bad.
Watch out, Hong Kong, here comes bilingual Ruth!

Let's go to Hong Kong Records!
There's a new Green Day CD out!
Records
Oh yeah! And a 古巨基 one too!

Who's that?
He's so cute. You'll love him.

He's a Hong Kong popstar, but not like the Big 4.

香港唱片
Hong Kong Records
ENGLI
中文
Who's the Big 4?
OMG. They are the best and cutest popstars.

andy lau
LEON LAI
There's Leon Lai and Andy Lau...

...and Jacky Cheung and my fave, Aaron Kwok.
7折 30% OFF

Ooh, he's cute!

Hmm. Which one to buy?

I'll take... um...both.

Hong Ko
Let's go down to the first floor.
To Bossini!

BOSSINI!
These would be so weird if I wore them in Australia!
Canada too!

JUMBO B GRADE!
But there's so much more cute stationery than in Toronto!
Sydney too. I mean, just look at all these erasers!

There's the cute guy from my building!
We should go say hi.

Hurry! That was so embarrassing!

3 HOURS LATER...
BOSS
Phew!

Whoa, it's 4 o'clock already! I have to head home.
Me too!

Let's trade CDs at school on Monday.
Totally!

bossini
See you Monday!
Bye!

Through Queensway Plaza...
HMV

...across the skybridge to Star Ferry...

...and to the shuttle bus stop.
If only I could stop sweating!

Park

That was so fun!

I can't even remember why I was so nervous in the first place.

I can't wait to see Mom's face when she sees I made it home in one piece!

I'm home!

Mui,
Gone to meet some friends. Back at 6.
Mom
Out again? Ugh.

This is turning out to be rather anticlimactic.

What would make me feel less...weird?

Guess I'll go out for a swim and cool off.
Going Swimm

12

Empty.
Yes!

The sky looks the same wherever you are...
I could be in Toronto for all I know.

After a whole month, Bonnie finally invited me over to her place, but I'm stuck going to another family gathering.
FORTUNE DIM SUM
I don't even like dim sum.

This is your mom's family, and therefore my family, and yours too.
There they are!

Family is important. And you'll get to know them.
I know.

Plus, you love egg tarts!
OK, yes. True.

OKAY. Just breathe.
No one will even be focusing on you.
Just blend in.

Hi!
Hi!

Good morning, Mui!
Good morning.

Hi...

Guys, please sit on either side of me.
Don't be so difficult. Sit with your cousins.

Enjoy!
Thanks.

Here, have a 鳳爪!

Be respectful. Try it.
What do you say to your grandma?
Thank you.

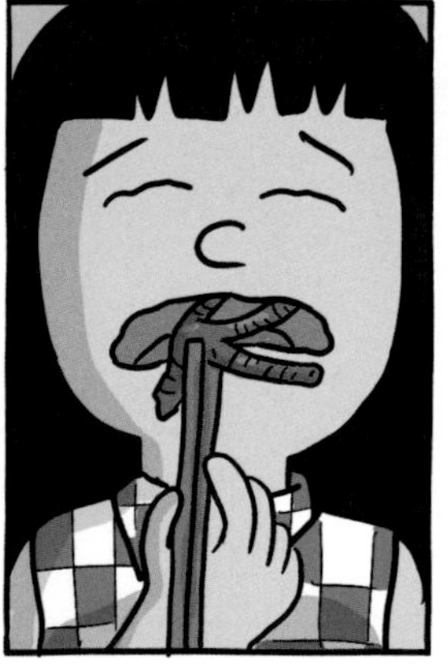

ALLOW

That was gross.
HA HA HA

HA HA HA HA HA

Oh! I'm not laughing at you!

I hate chicken feet too! That was cruel of her to give it to you.

Here, try my favorite: curry tentacles.
And this tripe.

Oh wait.

That's...GOOD!

See? Not so bad, right?
Yes. But please take the rest of this chicken foot from me.

Delicious!
Nap time?
我食到脹晒!

I'll pack that up for you!

Check, please!

No, check here, please!

Check!

CHECK!!!

Give the check to me!
It's...OW...
on me!
No!
I am paying!
No! My treat!

What is happening?!

Oh, this happens every time.

It would be my sincerest pleasure!
界面我, 等我埋单!
It's the Chinese way of saying how much you love each other. The more you insist, the more you care about them.
And this is a relatively mild version!

我要尊重長輩,
就等婆婆埋單.
Clearly, your parents raised you well.

Thank you,
Mother.

Thank you,
Grandma!

THANK YOU,
GRANDMA!

Thank you.
Next time,
I pay.

Thanks,
Mom,
and no,
I pay next.

Thank you,
Mom!

Thanks,
Grandma!
There's a
good girl.

That bill fight was
kind of hilariously
crazy, right?
Yeah!
It kind of was!
Trust me.
Just wait till
it's someone's
birthday!

Mui, take these leftovers.
Thank you, Poh Poh!

You should come over to our place soon.
Yeah! That'd be fun!

Bye!
Bye, cousins!

Well, that was fun.
It even looked like YOU had fun.
It wasn't a disaster.

Finally! A Talk-to-Talk!
I think it's been three weeks since our last Talk-to-Talk!
We could have one more if you weren't here for just ONE day!
Also, chicken feet are disgusting.

You would probably like them if you didn't know what they were.
Doubtful.

Anyway, last time we left off, they had just moved into the barn.

With the pigs!

Yes, with the pigs.

My family hadn't been there long before I was born.
I was two months premature.
He looks like a monkey.

Everyone had to adjust to make sure I survived.
He's hungry again, and I don't have any milk.
WAH! WAH!

There wasn't much of anything around.
We'll grind up rice and water for him to eat. It's all we have.

Wai Ming*, make sure to hold the umbrella still so dust doesn't get in his food.
*My aunt, dad's older sister

Things were looking so bleak...

Grandma's friends told her to let me die.

Save your energy for yourself and your other children.
You can always have another one after this is all over.

But your grandmother refused.
Absolutely not. You can leave now.

Many said she was stubborn, but really, it was that she had...

COURAGE.

PERSEVERANCE.

PATIENCE.

Yeah. This weekend felt like my patience and perseverance were kind of paying off.
I...went to the city on my own.
And I talked to Angie a little bit.

See? I knew you'd start feeling better about Hong Kong.
You've always had it in you.

Piano
CHAPTER 4
Hi guys!

8
Hi guys!
Sorry it's taken me so long to write again. It's been so hectic here! OK, like here is a typical day in the new life of Ruth:

I wake up at the crack of dawn every day to catch the bus.

Marcus is usually asleep on the bus.

Bonnie and I have nicknamed him "DBD," which stands for "Don't Be Desperate," but it doesn't really work. I'm desperate for him!

School is blah, but this thing happened in biology class the other day.

My kind-of-friend, Claudia, and I had to do an experiment.

We had to...

Chew this bread and spit a little into the petri dish every two minutes.

So we were chewing...

...and spitting...

...and then I was getting bored, so I made a funny face...

...which made Claudia bust out laughing...

...and she spat bread ALL OVER ME!

It was so gross but kind of hilarious.

When I get home, it's usually just me. Mom leaves me a note to say she's out with her sisters or her friends or whatever.

I always go swimming after school. The pool is HUGE and amazing!

And the other day, I met a new friend, Matt, at the pool. We actually go to the same school!

He's way better at doing handstands than I am, but I can hold my breath longer.

breath
Anyway everytim
phone rings I hope
BRING!

Hello?

It's me!

Bonnie! Hi!
Thank God, I thought you were going to be one of my dad's work people asking for him again.

OMG.
Here we go again!

Claudia said the same thing when I told her about how much I hate answering the phone. She was laughing so hard, it was borderline cruel!

Wait, who's Claudia again?

Anyway, I promised my mom if I was on the phone, it had to be for school. Want to do geography homework together?
Sure! And maybe our maths homework too.

"HOMEWORK"
"OMG, I just want to squish him!"
"He was wearing his leather jacket and he looked sooo cool."
"I'm thinking of taking up skateboarding."
"Did you watch the horsey show yesterday?"
TOR

I know, I know. I knew this would happen. But forging friendships is more important than learning what a "wave-cut platform" is!

4:52

And you can pump air INTO the shoe. I got the last pair of pink ones...

I've got geography, math...I mean, maths, and German homework, but it's only 5 o'clock.

5:02

...What are you going to wear to school tomorrow? I'm going to wear the new Bossini shirt we both got at the mall, I think!

OK, I can totally talk a little longer and still get my work done.

5:35

...and I'm thinking that maybe I'll

CALL WAITING BEEEPP

Hello?

Why are you answering the phone in Chinese?
Oh, it's you. Hello, brother.

Yeah, OK, I miss you too. I just need you to tell Mom and Dad that I need to get a new cello bow. But otherwise, I am all good here. Actually, better than good, it's awesome. I basically just hang out with my friends 24/7!
YAWN

Cool cool cool. Everything's great here too. You're missing out on a lot of loud talking when Mom's with her family.
Now we know why she talks so loud all the time!

OMG. You have NO idea!

HA HA HA HA HA!
HA HA HA HA!

Man, I forgot how nice it is to laugh with Goh.
Hey, I've been meaning to ask you about the baseball card. Did you mean to leave it for me?

Oh shoot, I gotta go. Someone else needs the phone.
OK, cool. I'll tell Mom about your bow. Byeeee.

I should probably get started on this homework.
Ugh...so, what's a "wave-cut platform"?

These past few weeks feel like they're flying by.
Hi, Bon Bon. What's up?
Oh hey, Claudia, how's it going?
Swimming now? Yeah! Meet you downstairs in five minutes!

School is still...school.
...and we'll have a quiz on all this next week.
Scribble scribble

Why does my bag keep feeling heavier and heavier?!

We still have 45 minutes of class?!
Blah blah math equation thingies blah blah.

I guess it's got its highlights too.
A new drink machine!
Ooh!
So many options!
LEMON TEA

Ugh, I'm short 50¢.
You can borrow. Here's $1!

You guys in line?
N...uh...
No, we're done.

OMG. Marcus talked to me.
Kind of!

Even the weekends feel busy.

Isn't it great that Angie's family is inviting us to celebrate the end of lychee season with them?

Uh-huh.

Welcome to our home! And our backyard!
THAT'S the lychee tree? It's huge!

Yeah, and we have to pick them all today!

Six bags!
Have you ever seen so many lychees?

And now the weekend is already over.
OK, that's enough lychees for today.
PAT PAT

Why can't weekends be four days long?
Here goes another week.
9:34

THE NEXT AFTERNOON
Phew, that chemistry quiz was tough. My brain hurts.

And geez, I need to catch up on *Lord of the Flies*. I could barely follow anything in class today.

But first, a swim!

Oh hi, Hannibal!

Hi, my sweet boy.

WIPE
WIPE
Hi...Mom? You're home?

Oh no. Something is definitely up.

So. I got a call from your school today.
Okaayyy.

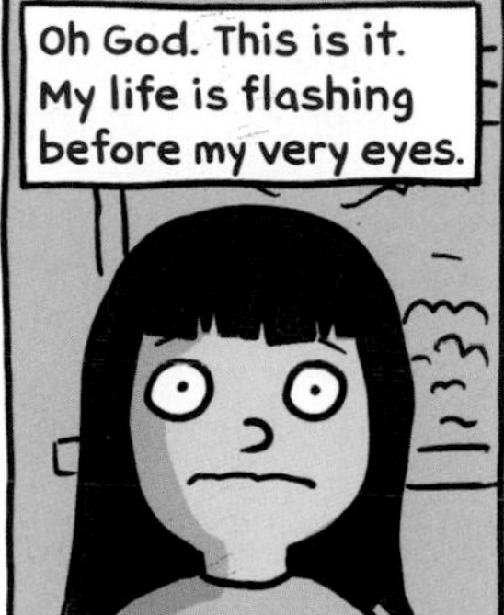
Oh God. This is it. My life is flashing before my very eyes.

IN MY MIND
ACTUAL
They called with concerns about your academic performance. They said you could be doing better. And that you aren't really trying.
I...

I am so disappointed in you.
It's been hard to...

No excuses. My friend's daughter Jane moved here the same time we did, and she is running for class president!

OMG. Here we go. Why does she always have to compare me to someone else?
And her sister got into Intermediate German already.

Holy guilt trip. Holy shame trip!
And you're prioritizing the wrong things. Always on the phone or writing letters.

Why are grades the only thing that matters to her?

And why is she always focusing on the negative?

And why does she have to rain on my parade, just as I'm starting to feel good about things in Hong Kong?

She's too busy enjoying her fabulous life here to even wonder how I've been feeling.

Ugh. I miss Dad.

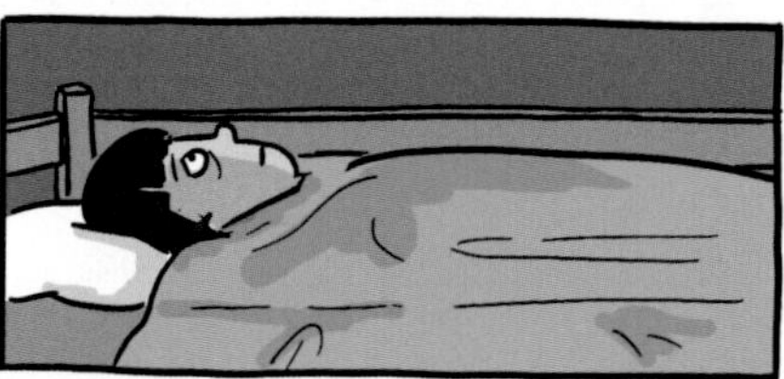

8 HOURS LATER
BEEP BEEP
BEEP BEEP

Drink your Essence of Chicken!
Okay.
GULP
This stuff is so gross.

7

Well, that was a rough 12 hours.

I wonder how long
I can go without
talking to Mom.

SMACK

Sorry about that.

HERE YOU GO!

Thanks.

Wait till Bonnie hears what just happened on the bus...
DEUTSCH-SCHWEIZERISCHE INTERNATIONALE SC
GERMAN SWISS INTERNATIONAL SCHOOL
德瑞國際學校
...and how unfair and ridiculous Mom was.

Hey, Bon!

Anyway, so then...

For real. I have to tell you about Marcus...

...and my mom...

HA HA HA HA HA HA HA

Um...okay...

Have you guys seen Claudia?
Nope.
I heard she's out sick today.

Ruth!
Watch out!

Bonnie acted like she didn't even know me.
I wonder what I did wrong.
Is it because I didn't seem to care about her sneakers?
Is this shirt not cool anymore?
Did she find a new best friend who is more like her?
Who is more Chinese?
Hmm. No Matt either.

I miss my old friends.

They'd never be like this.

I even miss my old school, where it wasn't all about studying...

...and where I could just be...me.

COURAGE.
NOPE.
PERSEVERANCE.
NOPE.
PATIENCE.
NOPE.

Hannibal?

Kitty?

Mom?

This is weird.

But she ALWAYS leaves a note.

Maybe she forgot?
I wouldn't be surprised.

OR MAYBE SOMETHING HAPPENED?!

It's not like Mom to forget to let me know where she is.
What would I do if something happened to her?

I need to do something.
Who can I call?

Ugghh.
Here we go.

RING
RING

Hello?

Hi, Poh Poh. It's, um, Mui. Is...my mom at your place?

喂，講大聲啲啊, I can't hear you. Who is this?

HI, POH POH. IT'S MUI. IS MY MOM THERE?

Oh! Hi, Mui! Your mom's not here, but your cousin Angie is. Do you want to talk to her? I haven't heard from your mom today and...

OK thanks bye.

SLAM!

Elaine - 883-5701
Wilkin (China) -
86-757-2993-0124
(office)
86-137-1538-6567
Lilian - 882 5923

Pick up, Dad. Please pick up. Please, please, PLEASE!

Where IS everyone?

And Goh is asleep...

TICK TICK
TICK TICK
TICK

HUMMMM

I've got...no one.

I'm so tired.

Tired of trying.

Everyone is where they're meant to be.
Except me.

1547

Mui! There you are! Guess who's home! We just got back from the airport!
And we brought home KFC for dinner!

Seriously?

Wow. They really have no idea.
Kentucky Fried Chicken

How am I not surprised.

OK.
Like fried chicken is going to solve everything?

WHAT did you just say?! You do NOT use that tone with us.

Whatever.

Dad is only here for one night.
Why are you being like this?

You are being
very rude.

STOP telling me what I am!
And I can't believe you don't even know what's wrong!
YOU DIDN'T EVEN LEAVE A NOTE!
I thought you DIED.

And who do I even call?!

My own best friend
won't even talk to me.

And my other best friends are
halfway across the world!

It's been AWFUL here,
and no one cares.

I'm expected to be brave and strong and good at school and magically fluent in Cantonese. And German? I'M NOT EVEN GERMAN!

And it's like everyone forgets about me.

No one ever asks me how I'm doing. I mean, you usually do, Dad, but you're never here.

It's always, "You should be more like this," or "Make sure you do this," and "Don't do that."

Like my feelings don't even matter...

It's...not that we don't care.

It's because we know you're going to be just fine.

BUT I'M
NOT FINE!

SLAM!

Kentucky Fried Chicken

CHAPTER 5

Just a classic teenager being miserable about life.

Floating through her day...

You can Save the World

Hey, Ruth!

What'd I miss
yesterday?
Oh man, am I
glad to see
you, Claudia.
Whoa, are
you OK?

Yeah, thanks. I had food
poisoning yesterday, but
I feel a little better.
My mom said I HAD to
go to school today.
Are YOU
OK?

Over here!

Hi!

I'm so full.

Check it out.

I see Ruth has the results we're looking for.

I should feel good about that, but...

Oh right, Dad's gone for the week again.

Mui,
I will be back by dinner and will bring back your favourite noodles
-mom

Mui, Have a good week.
Let's have a Talk-to-Talk when I'm back.
—Dad—

Well, at least they remembered to leave a note this time.

A package.
For me!
Ruth Chan
88 Tai Tam Res
Hong Kong
AIR MAIL
par avion

AIR MAIL

KETCHUP
POTATO CHIPS
CROUSTILLES
To Ruth

RUTH!
!!!!!!!
We miss you SO MUCH!
School
been the same. Ms. Ford is still
super strict and Hasmig got a
for laughing in class
(I did! This is Hasmig!)
because Shaun put his
Shoes on the opposite feet out of
Sheer boredom. It was sooooo funny!
This is Olga. There are a couple new
girls but no one can throw a
Wish you were here!
Hong Kong is

Have you seen Nightmare Before Christmas yet? We keep saying how it looks like something you would totally love. We wish we could watch it all together!
SMARTIES
SMARTIES
Anyway, we sent along some things to remind you of us, and of
CANADA
including your favourite!
And also some cookies Steph mom made for dogs that Hannibal might like!

PLEASE write us about your life! It sounds way more exciting than ours, and there are definitely no new cute boys here. You're SO LUCKY!
Love you,
A. G.
S. H.

I know this is supposed to cheer me up, so why does it make me feel worse?

Sigh, I might as well start some homework.
PHYSICS

CLICK

WIPES
WIPE
WIPE

WIPE
WIPE
WIPE

Here. Eat.
you can save the World.

I'm sorry for yelling.

But I just really miss home.
Or...I miss Canada.

I'm sorry too.
For forgetting to leave a note...

...and for assuming you'd be okay.

Even though I still know you are going to be fine, I know it's not easy to get to the place of feeling comfortable.

I've been so busy, I should have been more sensitive to how you've been feeling.

I can feel myself floating outside my body. This is surreal.

Did she really just apologize? And acknowledge my feelings?!

POP!
Are you listening to me?

Eh? Yes! Of course I am.

You know, Hong Kong is MY home. The one I left 30 years ago.

My family is here.
My language is here.
你話好
唔好笑？
真係
笑死人！
And my favorite breakfast.
My favorite
music is here.
And some of my
favorite memories.

And you know what? It's really nice not to have to drive you everywhere!

Sometimes I worry that me not being happy and perfect here will disappoint you.
Don't worry about that.

Listen, when I moved to North America, it wasn't easy for me either.

People did weird things. Like, they showered in the mornings and not at night, so you go to bed dirty! I thought it was so gross!
Heh.

Yes, and you said...

I AM from this country!

I sure did.

But I couldn't say that. I didn't have the guts to say anything back.

Just speaking English was so embarrassing for me.

I was also too timid to say anything, even though I could understand it well enough.

I can't believe it never occurred to me that Mom would kind of get how I'm feeling.

I mean, I DID order food at the food court myself. IN Cantonese.
Sounds like you're going to order all the dim sum for us next time, then!

Even though Bonnie still isn't talking to me, I feel like things might be getting better.
Good morning!

Well...some things.
Don't forget to drink your Essence of Chicken!

I know I'm going to be okay.

Or at least less cringeworthy?! (Dear God, please!)

It's definitely quieter though.
. . .

Like, annoyingly quiet.
Fine, I guess I HAVE to do schoolwork now.
BIOLOGY
DEUTSCH HEUTE!

Are you studying?

A FEW DAYS LATER
OK, let's go.

What? Don't I have to STUDY?
Where are we going?

We're taking the bus.

STAR FERRY
And now the ferry?

Ferry leaving for Tsim Sha Tsui in two minutes.
Hurry!
I'm coming!

The city looks so different from here.
TWINKLING STAR

And now we'll go to one of my favorite dessert spots.

果汁
Are we going up all those stairs?
Just halfway!
LADDER ST

OK, fine. Mom's Hong Kong is kind of cool.
FILM
KODAK
This pudding is yummy. Dad comes home tonight, so we should bring some back for him.
Good idea! And some more for US!
砵仔糕
$25

Later that night...

MURMUR
MURMUR

Dad's home.

KNOCK
KNOCK

Come in.

Mui, are you awake?
Maybe.

Sleeping Mui will have to do...
So I heard you had a talk with Mom a few days ago.

Yeah.
It was kind of nice to hear her own experiences. It made me feel like maybe she DOES get me.

I'm glad. You know, we didn't grow up in a very communicative culture, and sometimes we aren't the best at...talking about things.

I'm sorry too.
For being gone so much, for not checking in more during our Talk-to-Talks.
It's OK. Everything just happened at the same time and kind of snowballed.
And Bonnie still won't talk to me.

Actually...I don't really want to talk about it. Is that OK?
Of course.

Why don't you tell me about the bandits? That's the best part of the story!

I was a month old, and we were all sleeping upstairs in the barn.
Except my dad, who was awake with a fever.

All of a sudden, there was a bunch of noise.
CRASH!
BANG!

Everyone woke up, but your grandfather told us to be quiet.

Then he took his clogs and snuck into the darkness.

He took a breath...

...and yelled and stomped his clogs as loud as he possibly could.

At that moment, dark shadows were seen running away from the barn.

That is so gutsy.
Gutsy runs in our family.

What do you mean?
You.

Uh. No.
I have never felt more uncomfortable and out of place in my life than here.

Sure, but look at all the ways you've changed. It looks like you've made good friends. Mom said your Cantonese is getting better. You've been exploring the city. All of that is A LOT!

I still feel like I don't belong here.

I know it hasn't been easy. But you're doing better than you think.

Okay. Fine. I believe you.

Good. You should. I'm your wise, smart father.
One more thing...

Okayyyyyy...

After the other day... it made me realize that my being in China so much wasn't working for our family...

...So I put in a request to my company today to be transferred to a closer office. Either here or in a city just an hour away.
Really?!
Really.

Z Z Z Z

CHAPTER 6

Make sure you have some of the mango.
Okay, thanks.

That was the best night of sleep I've had in ages.
Thank you.

Do you want to bring some fruit with you?
No thanks!
Bus is coming, have to go.

Okay! Have a good day at school!
Remember, you're doing great!
Yep!
Wow. They are trying SO hard.

On the bus to school, I thought about Yeh Yeh and how he stood up for his family.

It's time I stand up for myself.

Oh God. I am terrified.

Okay, Ruth. You can do this.

You have the right to know what's going on!

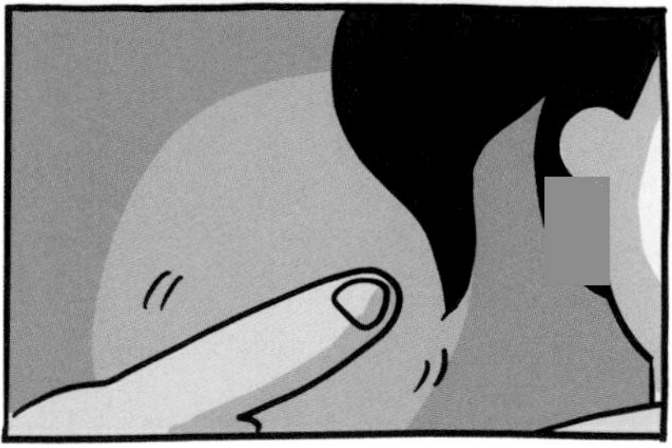

Um.
Can we talk?
Yeah.
Okay.

What's with the attitude?

So. What the heck is going on?
What do you mean?

You've been ignoring me for days. Did I DO something?!

It's just. Well. You and Claudia are always laughing and chatting.

And... Well... I...

Okay, FINE! I'm jealous, OK?!

Wait. WHAT?!
You guys are always having so much fun, and...I feel left out.

HA HA HA HA HA

No way! I was the one feeling left out! You were always hanging out with other people.
Because I was scared I wasn't cool enough for you!

HA HA HA HA HA HA HA HA HA
HA HA
HA
HA
HA

I'm sorry for not talking to you. I REALLY missed you.
Me too.

OMG. I have SO much to catch you up on! I might have to call you tonight too.
Uh, YEAH!

It turns out, November is kind of a good time to be in Hong Kong.

There's a great view up ahead!

It's also cool enough not to be sweating constantly.
There are so many of those soaring birds today!
They're up so high too!
40
KENNEDY TOWN
堅尼地城
TRAM

And it barely rains!
Are you guys paying attention?
...and then the cute guy from the 18th floor smiled at me.
OMG. No way!

It's still warm enough to do my favorite things outside...
(Angie lives outside the city with entire houses and quiet streets. Who would have thought Hong Kong had places like this.)

...with friends...
COWABUNGA!
OMG, too close!

...and on my own too.

Not gonna lie, though. The best part is the pre-Christmas SALES!

I'm so excited we get to shop all together!

I can't wait to get ALL the Japanese snacks!

Me too!

BOSS

And just like that, it's Christmas.
WELCOME TO HONG KONG
歡迎蒞臨香港

SMELLIEST
GOH!

The next day, Tour Guide Ruth is ready to rock and roll!

PUBLIC LIGHT BUS 16 CA
Hi! Thanks!

Okay, so we're going to take this minibus to Causeway Bay, but there aren't stops, so you have to yell out where we want to get off.

Ha! He looks straight-up nervous. Dare I say... overwhelmed?

Causeway Bay was Mom's favorite place to go growing up. You're going to love it.

Okay. So shops are open on Christmas Eve?
Duh!

Now to lead him into the belly of the beast.

$10
4件
$12
3件
$12
$8
$10
Two more, please.

JVC
CANON
LEICA
FM2
FUJI

Sasa
莎莎
CAUSEWAY BA
Hurry up, we're going to be late for dinner with Mom and Dad.

A,B,C

You've become a total local.

Pssh... So?

I guess I have in some way.

And it feels... good?

Stand on the right.

CHICAGO
DAN RYAN'S
GRILL
HONG KONG

JAZZ

Merry Christmas Eve!
How was Causeway Bay?
Mui wouldn't even let me stop for a bathroom break.

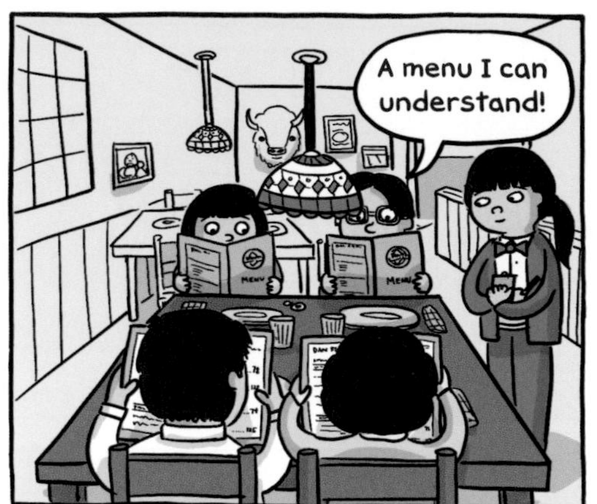
A menu I can understand!

Oh boy, have I missed this kind of food!
DAN RYAN'S CHICAG
Premium hamburger..
Chicago BBQ burger..
BBQ pork ribs .....
Homestyle lasagna ....
Seafood risotto .....
Classic mac n cheese...

Ooh. I'm so getting the lasagna.
Yeah, me too.
I'll have the cheeseburger, please.

The card!

By the way, I keep meaning to give this back to you. Consider it your Christmas present. Heh.
Nah, I left it for you on purpose.

Thanks.

Burgers are my favorite! It looks just as good as they make them in North America!

I can almost imagine we ARE in Canada.

Wait! I want to say something.
I know our family has been through a lot the last few months. I'm grateful we can all be together.

To togetherness!
To courage. And perseverance! And patience!
Wow. Deep.

UNIVERSAL SOLDIER
LEON LAI
SCHEDULE
古巨基
LEO KOO
We miss you
DEUTSCH HEUTE

OMG. Also, you have to try this thing my friend Matt (who I go swimming with all the time) showed me.

IT GOES LIKE THIS:

1 Melt marshmallow.

2 Unwrap Mars Bar.

rs

3 Dip Mars Bar in melted marshmallow.

4 Enjoy!

Let's make more!

It'll be Chinese New Year soon, and it's a pretty big deal here. We get a week and a half off school for it! And there's lots of celebrating.
FOOD
Steamed fish
turnip cake
DECORATIONS
福
MONEY!
(Lai See)

I MISS you guys!
Hopefully I can come visit at Easter or Summer holiday. Write back and tell me all the things that have been going on!
Love you!
Rut
P.S. Kitty and Hannibal say hi!

Mui! Time to go. The movie is at 3 o'clock!

Coming!

CHINESE NEW YEAR WEEK
恭喜發
年年有余
新年快樂
The whole city looks different!
新年快樂

輝永大廈 FAIR WIND MANOR
新年快樂
恭喜發財
Whoa.
Poh Poh's building
went all out!

Happy New Year!
Happy New Year!
福

出入平安
身体健康

四時佳興與人同
You're here!
Happy New Year!

May you have good health!
May you have happiness and prosperity!

I'm here.
四時佳興
萬物靜觀

公公
六姨媽
蝦舅父
婆婆
鉅舅父
大姨媽
蝦舅母
五姨媽
Wishing you good health!

I belong.

I'm home.
BOOM!
POP!

BANG!
FIZZ!

# AUTHOR'S NOTE

**IF YOU HAD GIVEN 13-YEAR-OLD ME A CHOICE WHETHER** to move to Hong Kong or stay in Toronto, chances are I would have said, "No way I'm going to Hong Kong! Why leave everything I know and love to start over somewhere so completely new and different?"

Well, we moved anyway, and like any kind of big change, it wasn't easy. Oftentimes it was straight-up uncomfortable and disorienting. One example: In Canada, people only saw me as Chinese, but all of a sudden, in Hong Kong, I wasn't "Chinese" enough because I didn't speak Cantonese well and dressed differently. Very confusing. I felt lonely in a new place, like no one understood me or seemed to care about how I was doing. It was hard. But the thing I didn't expect was how much I'd learn about myself by working through all those challenges, and how many of those experiences ended up being amazing and important ones. I learned to speak my family's language better. I made amazing friends I'm still close with today. I fell in love with a beautiful, vibrant, and unique city. I discovered so many sumptuous Chinese desserts, from bowl pudding cake to my favorite gooey Hong Kong French toast!

Writing this book felt eerily similar to that move to Hong Kong. I'd never made a graphic novel before, and everything felt new and scary. Originally, I had wanted to make a book about how my father was born while his family was on the run during the Second Sino-Japanese War. My grandmother and aunt would tell this story to my cousins and me every year growing up. It had become a Chan family legend. But the more I wrote, the more I realized why the story had always stuck with me. Just like my grandmother and her family, I had also been uprooted from all I knew.

I switched gears and started rewriting the book to tell both the myth-like story of my father's birth and my own story about moving. Sometimes it felt like I had no idea what I was doing, and there were days when I thought I'd rip my hair out and I'd have to go on a big, long walk with my dog. But just like when I moved to Hong Kong all those years ago, I found that unexpectedly wonderful things emerged as I struggled to make this book.

I laughed my way through hundreds of photos, (very cringey) diary entries, and even faxes (from when my mom forbade me from using the phone because I was spending too much time on it, so Bonnie and I sent faxes to each other instead). My parents and friends and I had long, intimate conversations about what we remembered from that time. I fell in love with Hong Kong all over again, and I got to look back and see how my time there shaped me into who I am today. Above all, I got to honor the incredible strength that my Mah Mah, my aunt, and my parents possessed in overcoming all the things that came their way, a strength I hoped had been passed down to me.

I still get nervous when I speak Cantonese, and I still don't like chicken feet. But making this book has helped me grow and has made me see, once again, how courage, perseverance, and patience can help you get through some hard times. It's amazing how adaptable we are as humans. Life isn't always smooth or in our control, and oftentimes we can't predict what's going to happen or how people will react. To top it all off, most things that help us grow and learn aren't easy. But if you reach out, stay open, give yourself time, and keep going, you'll find your people and you'll find all sorts of unexpectedly wonderful things waiting for you.

I hope this book helps you feel a little less lonely when you are facing something new or difficult, and reminds you that you are home wherever you are because of the people who love you and believe in you.

**RUTH CHAN** is an illustrator and author who spent her childhood tobogganing in Canada, her teens in Hong Kong and China, a number of years studying art and education, and a decade working with youth and families in underserved communities. She now writes and illustrates children's books and comics in New York City, and remains a proud Canadian.

**@ohtruth / ohtruth.com**